The Seventh Gesture

The Seventh Gesture

TSVETANKA ELENKOVA

Translated by
Jonathan Dunne

Shearsman Books
Exeter

This translation first published in the United Kingdom in 2010
by
Shearsman Books Ltd
58 Velwell Road
Exeter EX4 4LD

www.shearsman.com

ISBN 978-1-84861-084-2
First Edition

Acknowledgements
The Seventh Gesture was first published in Bulgarian as *Седмият
жест* in 2005 by Zaharii Stoyanov/Sofia University Press.

CONTENTS

Translator's Foreword

There are two things that are rarely talked about in childhood: sex and death. And this is why so many teenagers rebel, dye their hair, pierce their nose, become independent travellers, because there's a question they're too afraid to ask and an answer their parents do not know.

I have learned the answer, but it has left me stranded like a whale on the beach, it hasn't given me wings, as I expected, or it has but then it's placed me at the centre of a storm, under the net, and I only glimpse the silhouette of my freedom, like a butterfly on the wall of a roofless church, most of the time it's a burden, a weight I carry around. You see, we only begin to see when we learn that we are blind.

This was my experience translating this book, *The Seventh Gesture*, by the international Bulgarian author Tsvetanka Elenkova. I use the word 'author' lightly, for we are all translators, nothing begins with us, not even the life we give our children. We are called to translate and in the process to find meaning. Meaning is a tentative thing, open to interpretation. Do spiders fly, or do birds follow an invisible path? Is the experience of death akin to returning to the water from whence we came (a theory espoused by the Book of Genesis as much as by evolutionists, meaning again slippery, clothes turned inside out which no one notices)? This book taught me to find life in death, a dead tree bathed in light. This book taught me to follow the diffraction of light in a bruise, proving that we are indeed children of light (that teenager again before he dons a suit and tie and enters the world of make-believe). Or how about illnesses that come from outside and form a lump in our throat? Only after reading this book did I realise the storm has a face, a body, which tells us it's coming, like a scent.

Coincidence means things that happen together, not chance happenings. This is the only language I know and language, as any parent will tell you, is the ability to envisage the future, a dangerous gift, of course, like fire, but also beneficial.

I interpret coincidence and find meaning. A ladybird lands on the dashboard of our car I have seen before, again like a translation. I give it meaning and so I open my hand. To believe is to receive sight, but there needs to be some kind of catalyst, a revelation.

May this book (in translation—it doesn't matter whether you're reading it in English or Bulgarian) serve as a revelation, a gesture towards a country, Bulgaria, and its culture still unknown.

Jonathan Dunne

for my mother

The living ideal of God's love precedes our love and holds in itself the secret of its idealisation.

VLADIMIR SOLOVYOV, *The Meaning of Love*

Strong white resembles black.

LAO TZU, *Tao Te Ching*

POETRY'S TAIL

You wave the wand and know exactly where your wave will end. As the artist strokes a brush across the canvas, as the conductor signals *allegro vivace*, as the godmother turns the pumpkin into a carriage. You don't stop suddenly but smoothly, gradually tapering off. Which in time can be compared to wearing out a pair of shoes. Sliding away. Which in time can be compared to the same pair of shoes on ice. But what's most important—the curve at the end. The Bulgarians incorporated it into the buckles of their belts.

The Wounds of Freedom

Some buy leather leads for dogs of a definite length. Others prefer automatic leads with a reel. You let the dog run at will but you decide when to retrieve it. I set mine free. But two or three times it ran away and came back covered in wounds, so now I set it free but only in my yard. My dog howls at the squirrels, in the evening at the moon. And when we pile firewood next to the fence it climbs up and jumps over it. And again comes back with wounds. After that I decided to keep it on a chain. For my dog to be free of wounds.

MASOCHISTS

Because from an early age we endure pain. Except for birth perhaps, which our mothers bear. And that's why birth pangs are so strong. Until the walnut's husk darkens, until it hardens, until the green outer covering falls away. Until it no longer dirties our fingers. Until the bitterness loses its taste. Until many months, seasons go by and someone cracks open the walnut. Fallen before from your grandfather's sack. Because it is hollow—a real relic, the nut. From a metre sixty to a mere sixty. That's why we are masochists. Inwardly.

LIKE TICKS

Every day my cat brings in ticks. Normally on its legs or its most sensitive part, where all the arteries pass. Poppy-seeds, the ticks: small and black, but having drunk their fill, they blossom. I saw two—on the trunk of a date-palm in Rhodes and on a stone in Delphi. And all around drops of blood, all around whole puddles. Crushed ones. I look up and spy several black clots—olives. Who says, when we love we don't need another to feed us? As a mother feeds her child.

WITH WINGS AND TEETH

Where is the difference? Is it in the lack of plumage or of teeth? Only people, I think, are born without teeth and all their life hope for wings. Demons and angels must have created them. Some lose their teeth, others only have teeth left. If you're a treasure-hunter, you'll understand. But I never found anyone with wings. Only with *shards*, which tormented my grandmother and bent her double—dung-beetle. When we buried her with two lilies of the *valley*, when a grassblade *welled* up from the sprinkling, I saw them. Growing transparent.

BEETLES

I love beetles because of their two pairs of wings. Because they can be butterflies and bats simultaneously. They can cut with their wings and flutter. Be old women and young brides. The ladybird is my favourite. Because of the Orthodox principle in it (the many churches on its wings) and because it shows me the way. Or the way of my darling. Or maybe because it is part of a girls' game, a continuation of that children's game, in which you pluck the leaves on which it crawls and cleans up the greenfly: *'He loves me, he loves me not . . .'*

All's Well that Ends Well

'*All's well that ends well,*' says my mother and she puts the clothes in the washing machine face out. For them to *be clean.* She hangs the clothes on the line inside out. For them not to *bleach.* All's well that ends well, but how to know where the inside ends and the face begins? Children often confuse the two, madmen also. I once put my summer dress on the wrong way round and walked in the Old Town of Rhodes. Nobody noticed. They looked at my legs, some in my eyes. Is my mother right or do we just not see?

Change of Water Main

After a disruption in the network, there's usually a short circuit. The power fails. After a disruption in the water main, leaks usually start. Half runs through the tap, the rest is lost somewhere. You pay for it all. Everyone drinks the water from the tap. No one knows about the rest. They only imagine. Old stoneware pipes, reputed to give you cancer. They came, changed them for new ones. Three days we were without water. Now we drink it, we pay. It has a metallic taste. 'No one deserves a girl's tears,' my mother would say.

THE LAST WILL BE FIRST . . .

I started where I finished. With the last drops from the watering-can I watered the flower, with the first again. Those we planted out; the others, straight in the soil, caught up with them. The gardenia flower drooped like a flower on the chocolate icing. In the photograph you can't tell them apart. Only my dog in the whole house is a virgin. I hear it howling by night at the moon, I think it is howling at the moon's hymen. And it mounts the rugs when we take them out in spring. The rugs we wash in autumn. And wash again.

Driving Is Not for Everyone

When I am behind the wheel, scatty, wind under me as from the ventilator just inside a department store. Sometimes I feel how it holds me in its lane, ball for bowling, with my weight I feel it. But I cling to the wheel. I drive. The *volants* of my skirt pleated from turning. From remaining stationary. When I am behind the wheel. And I see coming towards me trees, fields, houses, others like me. In a revolving *wheel*, from which the winning numbers are drawn in a lottery. Scatty as I am, someone reaches out and snatches me.

IN THE SCHEME OF THE COSMOS

When you enter the track, keep going. Don't stop at every station. Be like an express, like a water-slide, but not at its beginning and end. Your speed must be measured. That's why there are tunnels, covered water-slides. So that you don't fly off. Except for birds, only aeroplanes can fly—and *spiders*. Not trucks for lifting cars, but which drop from the ceiling to the floor of our rooms. They make their own tracks and these are invisible. That's why we talk about flying. Even birds follow a path. In the scheme of the cosmos.

HALL OF DISTORTING MIRRORS

Every fair has its hall of distorting mirrors. The extended projection of the Parthenon, asserts Seferis, is a pyramid. Reflected, the pyramid looks like an ellipse, and the lemon-tree in my yard with the five tips is probably a circle. Albeit not ideal. So many edges, shapes, images, points of glass, you'd say, so jagged, why reflect them? Why iron clothes that should be worn creased? Natural edges cannot be smoothed out, even with steam—from a combination of moisture and sun. From agitation. You wipe the mirror. For a rear view.

Men's Ties

Unless they're called up, men wear suits with a shirt and *tie*, whatever the season. They don't have much choice. Unless they wear jeans. Their shirts of knights, their *ties* from the time of Judas, Ariadne, the first man (or his soft rib), from Genesis. Apart from their *ties*, men don't have other prospects. *Ties* for shirts, shoes, belts. They never take them off. Their fathers' rosaries—one by one, the beads through the fingers, why not, to kill time. You can't say if they swoop or roll.

TIME

Time fills with words *drop after drop* like a sink with the plug in. Time also has an overflow. Two or three who couldn't bear it and left. A few stayed behind to measure time. Some fidgeted on their chairs, handed each other notes, whispered in their neighbour's ear; girls lifted air with their skirts, not having aprons as their grandmothers did. Others listened carefully (you'd say they've an exam soon) and took notes. In the hall it was stuffy. *Drop after drop* trickled down their foreheads.

Sixty

You wind the car and set it down on the carpet. Towards the end it *whirrs* fast *whirrs*, just before the water collected in the spout runs out. Drops not like those of stalactites, centuries to accumulate in one spot, but like a pulsimeter, turning idly. Like the first, faltering steps of a child, making a beeline for its mother. How it laughs at the car and claps its hands—one, two, three times. The car *weaves* fast *weaves*, especially when it encounters an obstacle, turning idly. 'Time flies,' my mother would say, 'after sixty.'

There Is Life in Death I

My mother doesn't hear me because she's very old. Dead skin covers her entire body. Like snakes before they slough off the old. Even if you cut it with nail-clippers or burn it with salicylic acid, she doesn't feel a thing. She sits on the stone all alone, waiting for no one. Her bare feet covered with scales from wearing uncomfortable shoes. Blotches on her hands, her face (they may even be gills). My mother has difficulty breathing on dry land. She changes the plasters but the corns grow in. They still grow. *Black spot in dead skin.*

THERE IS LIFE IN DEATH II

As leaves fall in autumn, someone chops down trees, stacks
them next to the stone wall, someone builds a fire and pokes
the yule-log, later brushes the ash—just a few embers in which
to bake potatoes; as the river sweeps up trees, having burst
its banks, and deposits them on the stones; as in spring the
autumn leaves are different—dry, bone dry, brittle, scratching
nails; like the relics of saints, Thracian warriors in the museum
—limestone in a child's coffin: so death also dies.

SMALL STATIONS

Like shadows we must be, stretching under the street lamps or under the slanting rays of the sun, starting from the feet but also from above—we are our own way. We must share the light but not stop, go on. Not the end but the direction is important. And when we sit under a vine, whose dappled shade so resembles the dawn and dusk, birdsong, a dog's bark, it must be a stone along the way, where we sit and rest. Such stories of life and death! The arrival is like those small stations at which the train stops for no more than three minutes.

It's Dawn Outside

It's dawn outside. I shall open to let the birds in. I shall switch off the light. I shall finish writing. I shall close my eyes and doze. A longing for rest, for the night, but as the ostrich buries its head or the chick under the brood-hen's wing. From fear. A longing for rest, for the night, but without the insolent midgets, mosquitoes, moths. I shall open to let the birds in, as one circled all day under the eaves, pecking from the cardboard box with bread for the dog. The crumbs of sleep, because a whole loaf is a lot for me.

THE DAY

The day dawns rosy as a baby's bottom. Soft and smelling of
fluff. With yellow around its mouth. And down on its little
head. Only one small cloud of saliva as it sucks. The day dawns
with birds cooing. Sometimes, if it's a boy, in blue. Nappies of
pure cotton. But we neither teach it nor mimic it. We do not
give it rattles or teething rings. The day, lonely as an abandoned
baby in front of an orphanage, waits for someone to pass, to
take a fancy to it, finally to show it on the news. Let's hope the
parents have it back.

Inanimate Nature

Physics is a lie. Everything about inanimate nature is a lie. While I was weeding my strawberries, I could feel the rain approach with a waft of its cool body, with the wind. I made haste. Some grasses I removed easily—milk teeth. The roots of others broke—molars. Some mingled with my strawberries—they're weeds as well. To pull out the grass you must get a good grip on it. And the rain kicks in. Ice-pack or anaesthetic, which passes slowly. When I come to, stones have grown and more grass.

ILLNESSES

As the moon raises the oceans, so illnesses come with their younger sisters, pains. From beyond. Forces that gather our bodies, organs, beat them and lay them out again. As a tornado the fences, houses and trees. The following morning the earth dishevelled, the earth ill with measles. As winter grit dashes against our faces in summer. And they burn as in a fever. And then people go out, sweep the yards, wash their hands and build fires. This is how earthquakes happened. With a drill on the teeth and without anaesthetic.

Passport Photos

Those severed heads in photos are not so horrific as in films. Although they're of our nearest and dearest and we carry them in our bags, sleep with them on the bedside table, talk to them. In the gloom of the church they are not horrific either—they say it's a holy place, far from all violence. It must be the lack of blood, but for the past and future. Only one with the crown of thorns and the closed-open eyes frightens me. Observing me from every angle. Only the woman who died in a car accident with a photo of Our Lady in her bag.

COLOURS ARE LAID IN THE DARK

At the beginning of every film, as at the end, there are several black frames where it is joined to the cartridge and to the spool of the camera so that it can rewind, so that it isn't exposed. While in the cartridge, the whole film is black. If it has advanced and you open it in the light, it also turns black. So sensitive on the road to Damascus or some other city. Colours are laid in the dark only with measured light. As much as filters through a straw hat or a pair of sunglasses. A flash. And when it's processed we look at the pictures.

The End of Old Films

On the island of Symi this summer I watched the vendors of sponges. How they sold some with big holes, others with pores only or untreated. They stuck them in various solutions to show how they whiten, then in water to show how much they hold. They kept some moist but most were dry like the stones lying around. When you made as if to buy, they always soaked it first and squeezed it out. Mine trickled water and dried quickly. The end of every love affair is like this, I think—like the black reel before *The End* of old films.

Humility Is Never Enough

When in the dark, before you enter the room, switch on the light—on the threshold itself—the pupil swallows the iris, its black swells not for the darkness but to let even the slightest ray through. When it is greedy like this, even lifeless: light to dark, more than a camera lens focusing on an insect on a flower. More than a photograph taken into the sun. And you close the *lid* then. You close the *eyelids*. Or someone else does. You're the seed of a plant that sows itself alone.

Olympics

When you flutter your eyelids, the air turns to silk. And
between two folds you see the unseen or hidden for a moment.
Red, muted light, the heart of a candle, the chink of some
door, through which it flickers, a waft and rustle of fingers on
whitewashed walls, of a wattled house in an earthquake. You
see those paper lanterns in front of Chinese restaurants with
painted flowers and dragons, how they sway. Then come the
voices, steps, shudder—echo from a team in a stadium. Only
their faces are missing.

THE SCENE IS IMPORTANT

While I watch how my son recounts a film, how he recollects
and pictures, his eyes fixed on one point, his eyes roll, dart, that
quarter in the night before waking and on sleeping, headlights
or torches in the dark, the flame of a candle in the wind. And
someone cups their hand, we dip them, someone flicks to
one, not to waste the battery. Or it's just that there are lots of
oncoming cars this long winter's evening. The secret alleyways
in the Middle Ages, entering Glojene cave. I tell you—the
scene, always the scene. It's important.

My Son's Night Eyes

for Vesi

They say that windows are the eyes of houses but through some it's difficult to look in. Rain-spattered, poorly washed, with frosted flowers or scratched. Others with paint from the frames. However, I remember one evening, when the curtains were not yet drawn, they became a mirror. What they reflected on the inside they let out, sleek and opaque with that indeterminate colour of a reptile's body—or better of its skin, cast next to a stone. Like the difference in houses reflected in the water of a single harbour at two separate times.

Somebody Winks at Me

Where my father's portrait is, there was a blank wall, before that bricks, and long before that I do not recall or simply there was nothing. Rains may have fallen, the sun may have shone, a sea of barley may have swayed. The wind will have blown and fruits grown wild like the oranges on the streets of Athens. Squashed oranges, which used to be blossom, smelling perhaps of jasmine or bleach. I don't know what came before the spring. Whether winter or just a frozen puddle. Before my father's portrait, a sty forms in my eye.

Under the Victim's Nails

for my father, Stefan Elenkov

If skin has memory, as doctors maintain, it means the house
you leaned on last, the sea you swam in, have not forgotten.
Only my dresses have forgotten because I take them to be dry-
cleaned or wash them often. But our sea, which is so enclosed
streams can't reach it—the vertical wall under the eaves the wet
can't get to—they have not forgotten. Like a pelican's bill or
a camel's hump, they save the memory for a rainy day. Like a
victim's nails, which still keep hairs from a killer's skin.

The Spark in Us

There is a wire between the thighs and palate. A wire on which the organs are hung like laundry. Trousers with their two legs, corsets, handkerchieves of various sizes. In a gust of wind the line comes undone and they all fall down. There is a wire that conducts electricity, and at each end a small tongue. Sometimes there's a short circuit and the electricity board sends someone out. They open the door of the meter affixed to the wall, check the seals, you pay up. If you do not wish to pay, they lay your wire underground.

LIKES ATTRACT

The comb was indented from too much combing. Its teeth thinning. Because the hair was thick and difficult to comb. The hair was indented from too much combing. Its strands thinning. Because the hair was thick and difficult to comb. First the comb, then the hair were thinning. In the photograph they look so alike. Bone comb. Brown hair. Bunches at the side, white with age. Sharp-pointed with a parting in the middle, dividing them into two equal parts. Thick or sparse hair. Electrified. Like the comb.

When the Facts Speak for Themselves, Even the Gods Are Silent

Even if the gods are silent, I will trust you again. Like rape covering the fields of central Europe. Which no one sees or knows about, except for the farmers. But from an aeroplane, for example, you can sweep it all with a single glance. Even if the gods are silent, I will trust you again, like oil drawn from this same rape—which is not sunflower oil or olive or vegetable or palm. Even if I haven't tasted it, I will take after it, its yellow blossom—which is not gold or sickness. So low but from above so lush.

ORPHEUS AND EURYDICE

Of all who lied to me, I believed all, but you most. Who lied
to me the most. That part in hide-and-seek, when you pretend
not to see your little friend, your child. It's the same when you
let someone start or slip him a card. Then you shake his hand
and kiss him on the right (or left) cheek. You—out of love
for him. He—out of love for the game. In a similar situation
Orpheus turned around and also didn't *spy* Eurydice. Didn't
spy her. But she receded. They say, by the will of the gods.

THE TIME WE ARE TOGETHER

In the time we are not together, time sinks. Like a pressed piano key. Even though it emits tone, music. In the time we are together, time is silence. You do not even press the right-hand pedal, which doesn't give out a sound but sustains it. The time we are together is silent. Our hands interlocked as for prayer. You've already written the words I wanted to say to you. And I will write the words you have to hear. The time we are together is so silent in our absence you can hear only the rustle of one or two *leaves*.

OSIRIS AND ISIS

As I see it, so scattered among us all—a suddenly broken necklace or spilt rice—so shattered—crystal on tiles, glass from a stone—I think that we serve it, not the other way round. Or it also served us, but before it dispersed—drops of mercury or sand. We took our temperature with it, decorated our shelves, our necks, ate. Now we sweep it up, wipe the floor and rinse the cloth. That's all. 'In any situation,' I say to my son, 'wear slippers and wash your hands. For a piece not to lodge in you.' Of the Word.

DONKEY AND DOVE, THE WORD

Your love is the inside of a book. How it flutters and how humble it is! Pages that fall lightly. So well thumbed that the cover has curved outwards. Just like a donkey's saddle. Blackened, already worn. I stand in the highest place, I point with the *index* (the book's, of course) there, where the *quires* are *sewn, coupled*. The *cars*. And I look at the roads—spaces between lines—the houses—negatives of letters, always flat from above. A real labyrinth, should you enter. We release a dove in front of us to lead the way.

ATHENS, FIVE O'CLOCK

The afternoon the light was a soft nappy or newspaper frayed between the palms, I saw them—in the base of the triangle, in the centre—two pigeons in love. First they rubbed cheeks, interlaced necks, then one landed higher. I observed how they didn't even touch. Or how the one above watched over the other. The light broke up, not into colours, into sheaves just like the Erechtheion's fluted columns. The light gathered. That's why everything is made from marble. White. Not from precious stones.

Safety Valves

When I see how the air directly over a candle turns to liquid, how the air over asphalt when hot also turns to liquid, how the sea in the sun recalls heated asphalt (some say it's a mirage), I understand these tears in me, down below like a tree's peeled bark, up above like a pruned vine, are actually fire, which combined with air makes water. Only high up in the treetops, the crowns, where the breeze never ceases, only there are found clouds—white or grey stratus, or a heap of fire and water combined.

ADVICE FOR MY UNBORN DAUGHTER

'How can God be Father, Son, and Holy Spirit?' asks my daughter (and all who can't explain His three faces). 'Like a cherry-tree,' I say, 'when it blossoms. And it is tree, flower, and sweet-smelling. Like a woman,' I say, 'when she's in love. And she is soil, *cell*, and sweet-smelling. Like a man,' I say, 'when he loves. And he is stars, seed, and sweet-smelling. When one spring you look at the *Milky Way* with the first drop of blood in your knickers, you'll understand what God is. Then you won't want to wash it off. No, you won't.'

WHY THE SPIRIT CREATES MATTER

How sweet is this opening fruit with fingers, when the juice runs down your hands, when the flesh divides, not along the veins. There's nothing sweeter than biting into it, as you leave your painted lips on paper or on chewing-gum smeared all over your face. Nothing sweeter than this cleaving a watermelon with a blow on the ground and your teeth sink in. With pressure and pleasure. As we puncture and make confetti. To celebrate New Year. This digging out coconut, the white for cakes, after you drink its juice is what attracts Him.

Your Body, a Garden

Your body excited and limp at the same time, loose soil. A dug garden, which you do not tread on but work with your hands. You clear it of small stones, odd blades of grass, and smooth it with a rake. You make small pits with your fingers or with a special stick for planting. Then a few seeds in each hole (as with animals), later you water it and hope for fine weather. And that your dog won't trample it. Along the wall you plant creepers—a green fence. Which is normally perennial and grows even in your sleep.

I WANT YOU EXHAUSTED

I want you exhausted like a blue cloud which has just stopped raining, like a mature brandy, like a snail whose shell has been broken, which ever so slowly descends a steep slope, like laundry which dried long ago, like an old woman's mottled hands, I want you exhausted like a blue cloud hanging over me, as I wait at a red light and a warm spring breeze rises, melting the snow, sifting the leaves, and we sit in short sleeves at the café tables, I want you exhausted like a sliced liver.

Of Stones and Worms

The softest parts, which work by their hardness, finish first. The softest parts rot first. Those that give life *die* first. In their nature, their destiny. The diamond, the hardest and most transparent. The worm, the softest, lives in the soil. The diamond between her thighs, the worm between his, or the other way round. So useful when they drill your teeth, when they loosen the soil. Important for wind-up watches—*17 Jewels*—and for the life cycle. Which adorn us, which eat us. Which we cannot be without.

The Music of the Flesh

The flesh of some is resonant or it echoes. Smack a small child on the bottom and then an athlete's tense muscle. The flesh of others rustles—paper. When I stroked my grandmother's hand. And is transparent like rice-paper. Rice-water I drink for stomach pains. Rice-powder I apply to my body. But the effect is temporary. My skin doesn't become transparent, only the veins bulge. Varicose veins inherited from my grandmother. Rivers encircling my body, lactating breasts. Turbid rivers. Not an echo is heard.

ELDERS

Those foetuses in biology, downstairs in maternity, in formalin with fish-eyes and bodies sans bones, sans teeth, sans hair even, but fossils. Those soaked behind glass, red-brown in colour, toddlers in appearance, ever the curious, standing on their shelf, unable to climb up (or down) the stairs, you only have to touch their skin and it peels, that's why there are special creams—PENATEN—those dressed in Pampers, even if it doesn't show, with their string hanging down to the floor, we call them elders.

Of Flies and Monks

I saw a monk in St Mary's Church in Lindos. And as flies landing on windows rub their legs, front and back, like ants and beetles, like all insects, so he in his black cassock, without his hat, touched all the icons one by one, kissed them, then replaced his hat, crossed himself and entered the sanctuary. Only that in the morning they washed the glass of the icons and lamps, all day long they kept the doors open and there were no nets or swatters on the table.

By the Crown or Roots

'A tree can wither by the crown or roots,' my grandmother used to say, seated in a wheelchair, sheltered from the sun and wind. Some people in their cars career into the wind and sun, sunroof open, windows down, hands hanging out, thumping music, wheelchair sent flying. Slam on the brakes, skid marks, blow a tyre. And yellow in the pants, around the mouth, on the nose, as if you had smelt a flower. 'A tree can wither by the crown or roots,' my grandmother used to say, 'or by both at once.'

As in an Amphitheatre

Cemeteries are always out of town. On a small rise. Cemeteries are higher than the town but the wood is higher than they are. The wood with venerable trees, part of the mountain, a bridge or cradle connecting two tops. Some cemeteries are in the wood but the tops are always higher. So the best view is from somewhere in the middle, if you divide an amphitheatre into three equal parts, though the echo is loudest in the last rows. The rows are in blocks, of course. For anyone who's late or suddenly gets up to find their seat more easily.

WHITSUN EVE

I picked two or three sprays of rose, cleaned them of thorns,
threw the thorns on the grass. Only the leaves and flower
remained. The people are like grass, like waves, everywhere
covering the stones, they spit out the cherry pits and the
chocolate melts in their mouths. They uproot the grass and
throw it away. The twisted candles on my grandmother's grave,
a running sore. Among weeds and clover. In one of the holes a
caterpillar has made a nest but is also uprooted. There is more
grass than earth. We reverse out. One rose before us.

Poems' Funeral

Like a sudden whirlwind, poems come. Like lightning far off in the sky but touching the earth. And always caught in a season. The flurry of leaves, the short circuit with the wet grass. You know that they've been from the swept yards, from the flattened clover, from the scent of coriander. Sometimes you can even trace their tracks—two skid marks from slamming on the brakes, two cart-ruts in the mud lane. And a procession of people at the rear. And poems have their funeral.

My Brother Was Writing Poetry

While I was writing my verses, my brother was working on his boat. He carefully dismantled the seats. He upturned the boat, sanded it down to white (making the cherry-tree turn white). Then he took it to a master to be given a number, to pass the test more easily. He applied putty for hours, then an undercoat, the way people polish teeth against tartar or put plasters on grazed knees. He circled it and wondered what to christen it. He named it after the hero of his favourite film. While I was working, my brother was writing poetry.

Poets' Mouths

At a concert I watch their hands—on the piano, the violin, the double bass, the kettledrums, the flute. Like centipedes, their hands. They tickle you with their legs, fondle you, invade your delicate parts. At a poetry reading I also watch their hands— held out, hushed, some barely trembling, a *leaf* in the wake of a bird. In their hands a *leaf* is the day, several drops of ink to put it to sleep. Then I understand that the hands are not important but what they play with—the words of their *mouths*, the *mouths* of instruments, which never love.

Wisdom—A Purged Conscience

Even though some go to bed and fall straight asleep, they do not even dream or have nightmares; even though they wake up late, at midday, after the birds have stopped singing and the air has become stale—that break between going to bed and getting up, between a clear conscience and wisdom, when the skin smooths out, taut, the body retreats, like the sea, which the following morning has thrown everything on to the shore—we call it *Purgatory*. Then we let our children into the water. Stark naked. And we to one side.

THE KNOTS OF WINDS

Some things are like the inner threads of a shirt—frayed because we've worn it a lot—and others like the outer—they don't rub against our body but are damaged from the outside. Or when we wash them unreversed. We bear them, a sack of gifts or cross on the shoulder. Non-stop Christmases and Easters. We untie them but in fact they tie us, we hand them round but in fact they gather us, and vice versa, as if linked like a flowerpot with a pail of water when we're not at home. Or the knots of winds that gather only on deck.

CHERNI VRAH

At the summit. Just a little grass between me and heaven. Violets everywhere. The earth wet and warm, a hot compress, a loving body. It heals me all over. Stones everywhere. As in an Indian tepee before the sacred ritual of the pipe. Stones bigger than the rivers, even though they're not dry. An austere, not gentle beauty—you'll break a tooth. But gentle as well, because of the water. How lovely it is when someone rings the bell, when everyone rings the bell—not of the church but of the meteorological station—2290 m. closer to God.

THE OTHER MEDITERRANEAN

There are also such mountains with their black woods, sea foam that crashes deep under. Mountains, volcanoes with their craters, wide islands whose rocks are beaten by the same black foam. The houses are barely visible, Atlantis of old, grey all of them, like the sky in these parts—the bottom. Grey and green, which go together so well—our *Inhospitable* sea. Two tones darker and you call it *Black*. That's why they painted their houses like this. With one hope. And sheds, not shrouds, next to them.

Sweetness Is in the Sun

Sweetness is in the sun, bitterness in the soil. Like cucumbers, whose roots are not edible by late autumn. Unless you pickle them. Like apricots, peaches, cherries (those black ones)—what need of toffees? The taste of a tanned body before you've gone for a dip in the sea, before you've sweated on the road to the beach, early in the morning or in the gloaming, when you half-close your eyes, suck me, rend me with your fingernails, to get at the stone, this sun half over the hills.

SOLAR ECLIPSE

The moon is a rodent, taking the sun in its hands for the first time. As a squirrel holds an acorn in the branches of an oak. It bit into it once, twice—*old moon*—and threw it from a height. The day darkened in the same phase as the night when there is no moon. Several seconds elapsed—*new moon*. Then it began to grow again. An acorn quickly sprouting in the soil. *Crescent moon. Full moon.* In thirty minutes the sun walked the way of the moon in a month. And its light spread over the sea again. The lunar path, which sailors claim is endless.

ON THE EQUINOX OF DOUGH

You add flour to the mixture, too thin and with floating lumps, you add more, the lumps turn to dust, it's bountiful and golden—summer. Right now you can pour it into a frying-pan and see how it separates by itself when it's cooked, sun, but you carry on adding flour, you want to make bread. A moraine already but still you carry on (Easter cakes are the most difficult). You knead. Without flour. You knead. With air. The clouds gather and it starts to rain, the woods thicken in the fold, wolf's neck. And give shelter. Autumn has come.

SLAUGHTER

We're caves and run inside. Whether it's raining out or dry. We always run inside. Even more forcefully when torrents come. The underground rivers are many, I cannot count them all. Every single one salty. As is clear from the stalactites and stalagmites. From the white rocks. Rocks, did I say? They shred like Easter cakes. Stratified. We run most in the corners, where the jaws, the clavicles, join. And this smell of dampness, and this blackness, only thin out at the entrance. Bristle, which you scrape off with a knife.

SELF-SACRIFICE

Inside I smell of the taste of earth. Earth that a child bites, having fallen flat on its face. Earth that in the east they sprinkled their heads with in sadness. Earth that alone flies in the mouth, left over from winter, from the dusty summer, in the first spring days. I refuse to swallow it. I'm even afraid. I spit at length in the street, a smoker, I spit, although it's not the done thing. I rinse my mouth. But I still smell of earth, a scrap of food lodged between two of my teeth. I probe it at length with a toothpick, till it bleeds.

WITH A SHIRT ON YOUR BACK

Not as the Egyptians buried their dead—together with their cattle and cutlery, together with their servants. Not as the Hindus—together with their wives and family. Not as the Thracians—with their trappings and horses. Not as the Muslims—they slide them out of the sheet, run and don't turn around. But only *with a shirt on their back*, naked, stark naked, as they came. The whole shirt rots. The placenta, which is thrown out after the birth. The placenta, which falls from the newborn's back. And they snip the umbilical cord.

THE VEIL

That veil they lift from your eyes for the first time, last of all from your eyes they lift. That other veil they lift for the second time before many witnesses. That third veil they let down, full of people all around. The white veil you're born with twice and die with once, under which your eyes will be seen no more, whatever may follow. The veil our grandmothers wove for their dowry, for a shroud. Why is it black now on this woman's shoulders, why is it black only when we lose our neighbour?

LIZARD'S TAIL

These photographs along the spiral staircase are a little lizard's tail that came off. It's been pinned between the ground and first floor but the little lizard is long gone. Probably with a new tail it runs along dusty roads just in front of a car's tyres and along fortified walls, feeling your hand, the hand of thousands before you, the echo in the stone—this land shell. It runs through the grasses, three days' growth. They hide the prints of ancient animals. The clown between the rows in a circus, with the red nose and distinctive hat.

GOOD AND EVIL ARE AT ODDS

How many dandelion-clocks on the sea, lovers' letters—how many drowned loves. How many gulls with their passionate screams, cats in spring—how much hope and realised loves. Over my head while I swim. And at the same time I see their bellies, just like that bomb over Hiroshima, just like those spilled from fighters during World War II, in black and white films. And at the same time—little crabs with upturned bellies, swayed by the sea, with pincers folded on their chest, as of a sleeping child, as of the dead.

FREEDOM IS CLOSENESS

Those metres of the swimming pool, which you go up and down. The pool divided into lanes. Those metres of the shore, which you go up and down. The shore divided into bays. Those metres of the town, which you go up and down. The town divided into streets. And it grows, and it swells. Especially at night, when it tucks its head under its wing. But it never flies away, though it can. And you've beaten a small path there, where the grass doesn't grow. As under a walnut's shade. Is freedom. Not given, not taken away.

THE LEGEND OF NARCISSUS

Every evening he waited for her at the window. But he only
ever saw himself and left. Till one day he decided to wait her
out and stopped waiting. Leaning over the water, he flopped
and started swimming. Not like people with their head above
water but like fish. He came up for air once or twice, a dolphin
or a whale, and then he sank for good. With eyes ever open
inside the looking-glass. The rest carried on learning about
evolution—how creatures emerged from the water on to dry
land. The rest carried on interpreting the legend of Narcissus.

THE SEVENTH GESTURE

With finger on mouth, when you do not want to wake someone or the teacher walks in. He puts a finger to his mouth when he wants to quieten the class. Or he tells you straight to shut up. But what intrigues me most is the way it slides down, pulls away from the lips. After you've imposed the silence. Some just loosen their hand, others draw it out to point, others hold it longer like this. And a fold in the fingers, bliss from the tiredness of the unwonted gesture. This is how the Byzantine iconographers first painted them. The saints.

Day One—The Giving of Fire

Unlike the lighting of a matchstick—He doesn't bring it close to strike, to rub (two stones or wood on wood), but moves it away. He doesn't move it in flames but growing cold—a pot taken off the stove. He doesn't then blow it out, having lit it, but blows it into a blaze. As the fire is kept alive on Christmas Eve. As it's given at Easter—candle to candle. Not the stick's burning down is important but the flare from the stick. Not the stick He cleans His teeth with but the stick between His teeth. To stop Him biting His tongue.

Day Two—The Light in Us

Not only did the glass break, which you dropped and it diffracted the light into four colours, those pieces under your soles, but also your right thigh, which in your hurry you bumped against the side of the table and it turned first red, then blue, grew green and finally yellow, in days, not seconds. And it hurt you, although you didn't receive a fragment. And it was dark but you weren't afraid to go barefoot. Like a window, it cracked without shattering, not like the others, which flew about. Not the Snow Queen's mirror.

Day Three—The Dilemma with the Snake

The straw hat on your head, through the top of which the sun penetrates so strongly it blinds and is wholly contained in an opening no bigger than the nail of a little finger; the straw hat, on whose brim the light dwindles, made to cast a shadow, dark, distant from the centre despite its outline; the straw hat, which always begins to fray at the edge—see how a straw sticks out yellow and bent but stiff: is Yours. And instead of pulling out the straw, better to have pushed it back.

Day Four—Leonardo's Cross

They find dead victims like this, with legs outstretched and arms to the side. Children sleep like this in their sweetest dreams. Like this, hung on a hook against you, I writhe at your every touch. Of the hardened body, split open up to the throat. Like this, with open mouth, waiting for you to release the catch, to close it—a door banging in the wind. To tie it, as with toothache. To tighten the legs of the lamb after you've stuffed it. The legs of a young bride who wants to conceive. The difference between Leonardo's cross and Christ's.

DAY FIVE—THE NATURAL *SIEVE*

Children on the beach most like playing with a *sieve*. They scoop with a little spade, tip, and set aside the big pebbles. They make a small heap. The rest falls and again they scoop, ever more deeply. The *sieve* has tiny holes, especially for sifting flour. Then, however, what's big is discarded. It's difficult for me to say, when there are wars, whether my son is sifting or my mother. I only know that this is a preliminary action. And actually sand is the natural *sieve-Christ* of the rivers we drink from.

Day Six—The Crucifix

When you embrace with such a wide embrace that it holds nothing back. When you serve soup in a dinner-plate so that it overflows for the dog or cat. When your palms in prayer become the profile of the Cross, or the Cross the full face of your palms. And there is no difference between joining and opening. Between the flame and the dripping wax. When you consider the symbols behind the symbolism, then you've understood what humility and ecstasy are—the profile and full face of a Picasso. Or everything that thins when stretched.

Day Seven—Birthday

Ever since I first sucked my mother's breast, I've always seen circles with a dot in the centre. The Buddhists' symbol, the eye of the Egyptians, even the Cross. You join three of its rays in a circle. With the fourth you stick it in the ground. Like a birthday candle, like a tree. To have a way to come down and to climb up. Finally to have something to lick. Some only lick their lips—dogs waiting for crumbs from the table. But to blow out the candles you must bend down. The candle right in front of your heart. *Many happy returns!*

www.ingramcontent.com/pod-product-compliance
Lightning Source LLC
Chambersburg PA
CBHW022205080426
42734CB00006B/562